50 FANTASTIC ESSAY

PRANJAL BORKAR

Contents

Contents

CHAPTER ONE

MY MOTHER

My mother is not an ordinary person; she is like a superhero. In every step of my life, she supports me, encourages me, and helps me make the right decision over time. At every time, she stands by and with me. Her contribution to my life is remarkable, and I can't express it through words. She had come with all the impressive dedication and conduct with some great inspiration over here. So, her contribution to the ultimate development of my life is remarkable for sure.

Through this fantastic My Mother easy, I would like to focus on why my mother is special to me, and not only my mother, every mother in this universe is special to her children. All their contribution and fascinating guidance made up proud and help us in taking all the super-efficient steps in handling all the super classy decisions over here. When we feel alone, then it's only my other hand that comes to me to support us.

She taught me the morality of our life. Yes, I got to know many things through her guidance, including

how to talk, walk, and take care of myself. My life is due to my mother. Her selfless contribution to my life is quite unbeatable in that she has helped me in improving myself.

Yes, 'she is my superhero,' and I mean it. All the efficient love and care towards me are excellent. She had brought a decent idea and comprehensive appearance to us. The overall well-being will make all things pretty clear and supremely perfect.

She taught us all her skills and the things that she had learned with the period. So, the contribution of her to us like supremely remarkable for sure.

It's pretty impressive to get all the fascinating experiences. The overall thinking and problem-solving thinking have supremely impressed me. So, this will make all the things efficient and unique to me. In this way, it brings all the effective services.

In simple words, it's pretty hard to explain the contribution of my mother to my life. She has done everything pretty clear and supremely excellent, so the overall fascinating criteria and selflessness make mother a beautiful soul.

CHAPTER TWO

MY FATHER

As everyone likes to believe that their father is different, so do I. Nonetheless, this conviction is not merely based on the love I have for him, but also because of his personality. My father is a teacher and is quite disciplined in all aspects of life. He is the one who taught me to always practice discipline no matter what work I do.

Most importantly, he has a jovial nature and always makes my mother laugh with his silly antics even after 14 years of marriage. I completely adore this silly side of him when he is with his loved ones. He tries his best to fulfill all our wishes but also maintains the strictness when the need arises.

One of the best things I love about my father is that he has always kept a very safe and open home environment. For instance, my siblings and I can talk about anything with him without the fear of being scolded or judged. This has helped us not to lie, which I have often noticed with my friends.

In addition, my father has an undying love for animals which makes him very sympathetic towards them. He practices his religion devotedly and is very charitable too. I have never seen my father misbehave with his elders in my entire life which makes me want to be like him even more.

My Father is My Source of Inspiration

I can proudly say that it is my father who has been my source of inspiration from day one. In other words, his perspective and personality together have shaped me as a person. Similarly, he has a great impact on the world as well in his own little ways. He devotes his free time in taking care of stray animals which inspires me to do the same.

My father has taught me the meaning of love in the form of a rose he gifts to my mother daily without fail. This consistency and affection encourage all of us to treat them the same way. All my knowledge of sports and cars, I have derived from my father.

To sum it up, I believe that my father has it all what it takes to be called a real-life superhero. The way he manages things professionally and personally leaves me mesmerized every time. No matter how tough the times got, I watched my father become tougher.

CHAPTER THREE

MY BROTHER

I have a younger brother, whose name is PRATHAMESH. He is eleven years old and studies in Class 5. My brother is cute and adorable. He is kind and polite by nature. We both love to spend time with each other. He is an intelligent kid, and everyone likes him. His favourite game is chess. We go to the same school and always have lunch together. He likes to share his secrets with me. I love my brother and hope we always share this amazing bond.

Our favourite indoor game is Carom. Evenings are always fun with him. His funny gestures make everyone happy. Being the youngest member of the family, he is the apple of everyone's eyes. prat hameshhardly gets angry. However, once a friend of mine was mocking me, and prathamesh came to my rescue. That was an instance when he was furious.

His thoughtfulness makes him a wonderful person. He is the sweetest younger brother. I honestly cannot imagine growing up without him. prathamesh has many friends. In school, he has always been popular.

However, he loves to spend time alone. At home, I would often catch him reading comic books. He also likes to draw cartoons. He loves to watch animated movies. Finding Nemo is his favourite movie.

His other hobbies include gardening. he has always been a gentle kid. He has a caring personality. While watering the plants, he would often sing a lullaby. Besides this, he loves eating tasty food. We always go to the nearby store and get ice creams. He also is a big fan of chocolates. The relationship between my brother and me is deep and special.

It only grows stronger with time. There are occasional fights and arguments. But at the end of the day, prathamesh and I are always looking after each other. Having my little brother in my life is an amazing gift. Being an older sister, I am responsible for his well-being. I try my best to keep him happy and positive. I love my brother. I wish he gets all the happiness he deserves and more. He is my hero.

CHAPTER FOUR

MY PARENTS

My parents are my strength who support me at every stage of life. I cannot imagine my life without them. My parents are like a guiding light who take me to the right path whenever I get lost.

My mother is a homemaker and she is the strongest woman I know. She helps me with my work and feeds me delicious foods. She was a teacher but left the job to take care of her children.

My mother makes many sacrifices for us that we are not even aware of. She always takes care of us and puts us before herself. She never wakes up late. Moreover, she is like a glue that binds us together as a family.

Parents are the strength and support system of their children. They carry with them so many responsibilities yet they never show it. We must be thankful to have parents in our lives as not everyone is lucky to have .

While my mother is always working at home, my father is the one who works outside. He is a kind human who always helps out my mother whenever he can. He is a loving man who helps out the needy too.

My father is a social person who interacts with our neighbours too. Moreover, he is an expert at maintaining his relationship with our relatives. My father works as a businessman and does a lot of hard work.

Even though he is a busy man, he always finds time for us. We spend our off days going to picnics or dinners. I admire my father for doing so much for us without any complaints.

He is a popular man in society as he is always there to help others. Whoever asks for his help, my father always helps them out. Therefore, he is a well-known man and a loving father whom I look up to.

I love both my parents with all my heart. They are kind people who have taught their children to be the same. Moreover, even when they have arguments, they always make up without letting it affect us. I aspire to become like my parents and achieve success in life with their blessings.

CHAPTER FIVE

MY FAMILY

Families are a blessing not everyone is fortunate enough to have. However, those who do, sometimes do not value this blessing. Some people spend time away from the family in order to become independent.

However, they do not realize its importance. Families are essential as they help in our growth. They develop us into becoming a complete person with an individual identity. Moreover, they give us a sense of security and a safe environment to flourish in.

We learn to socialize through our families only and develop our intellect. Studies show that people who live with their families tend to be happier than ones living alone. They act as your rock in times of trouble.

Families are the only ones who believe in you when the whole world doubts you. Similarly, when you are down and out, they are the first ones to cheer you up. Certainly, it is a true blessing to have a positive family by your side.

My family has been always by my side in ups and downs. They have taught me how to be a better person. My family consists of four siblings and my parents. We also have a pet dog that is no less than our family.

Within each family member, lies my strength. My mother is my strength as I can always count on her when I need a shoulder to cry on. She believes in me more than any other person. She is the backbone of our family. My father is someone who will always hide away his troubles for the sake of his family.

He has taught me the real meaning of strength. My siblings are my best friends on whom I can always fall back on. Even my pet dog has taught me the meaning of loyalty. He always cheers me up whenever I don't feel good. My family is my power that keeps pushing me to achieve newer heights.

In short, I will forever be indebted to my family for all they have done for me. I cannot imagine my life without them. They are my first teachers and my first friends.

They are responsible for creating a safe and secure environment for me at home. I can share everything with my family as they never judge one another. We believe in the power of love above everything and that drives us to help each other to become better human beings.

CHAPTER SIX

MY GRANDPARENTS

Grandparents are blessings from God who are irreplaceable. They are angels in disguise who are always looking over their kids and grandkids. As the times are evolving, people are losing touch of their tradition. Likewise, people are not realizing the importance of Grandparents. We see how they are mistreating them. While this happens in some cases, in most cases people love their grandparents.

Grandparents are truly a blessing in our lives. They are the ones who have made our parents the way they are. It is because of their upbringing that our parents love us immensely and care for us the same way our grandparents did when they were children. Moreover, grandparents are your support system. They are sometimes the only people who support you even if our parents don't.

Most importantly, grandparents are true believers in our skills and talent. They are the ones who push us to pursue our dreams when the world puts us down. Even though some of our dreams may not make sense

to them, nonetheless, they still believe in us. They boost our confidence and allow us to perform better.

Furthermore, grandparents are one of the main reasons why we feel safe and protected. We know even if we don't live with our grandparents, they are always praying for us. They are looking out for us. Almost everyone's safe place is their grandparent's home. We have a sense of calm and composure knowing we can always go to our grandparent's place if the need arises.

my grandparents always embraced me with open arms. They used to wait for every holiday for our arrival. My grandmother made delicious pickles and meals which we relished greatly. She taught me a few recipes too and tips and tricks that are very useful even today. I simply adore my grandparents for instilling good values in me and my parents and for giving us a safe space to grow up in.

CHAPTER SEVEN

MY SCHOOL

We have all been to school and we have loved each and every moment we have spent over there as those were the building blocks of our lives. A school is a place where students are taught the fundamentals of life, as well as how to grow and survive in life. It instils in us values and principles that serve as the foundation for a child's development.

My school is my second home where I spend most of my time. Above all, it gives me a platform to do better in life and also builds my personality. I feel blessed to study in one of the most prestigious and esteemed schools in the city. In addition, my school has a lot of assets which makes me feel fortunate to be a part of it.

my school name is podar international school washim.I LOVE MY SCHOOL I like my school due to its beauty and all over there are plants planted in a manner that we should fell pleasant while studying really when l go to school l fell very happy that today l am going to learn something new that will be intersting my each and every teacher is best one now is bad for me all the teachers treat me increadibly and l also love each and evry teachers teaching .

Teachers have the power to make or break a school. The teaching staff is regarded as the foundation of any educational society. It is their efforts to help kids learn and understand things that instil good habits and values in their students. While some concepts are simple to grasp, others necessitate the use of a skilled teacher to drive the home the idea with each pupil.

In contrast to other schools, my school does not solely focus on academic performance. In other words, it emphasizes on the overall development of their students. Along with our academics, extra-curricular activities are also organized at our school. This is one of the main reasons why I love my school as it does not measure everyone on the same scale. Our hardworking staff gives time to each child to grow at their own pace which instils confidence in them. My school has all the facilities of a library, computer room, playground, basketball court and more, to ensure we have it all at our disposal.

CHAPTER EIGHT

MY FAVOURITE GAME

If you want to be fit and physically healthy, the games are crucial. There are many games which I like to play, but football is my favorite game. The football is an outdoor game played by players of two teams. Both football teams have 11–11 players, which means that there are a total of 22 players in a football match. The team scoring the most number of goals is the winner, and the team with the least goals is the looser. In this game, a ball is played by kicking it with the foot. The game is also called Saucer in some countries. There are many forms of football tournament such as – Football Association (UK), Gridiron Football, American Football or Canadian Football (in the US and Canada), Australian Rule Football or Rugby League (Australia), Gallic Football (Ireland), Rugby Football (New Zealand) etc. Various forms of football are known as football codes.

Football is the most famous sport in the world, even in this modern era. It is a very thrilling and challenging game that is usually played by two teams for the enjoyment and entertainment of the youth. It is also played in front of judges to win or receive a prize on a competitive basis. Initially, it was played by villagers (called rugby in Italy).

There is a small area near the goalpost. 'D' is the game of that area. The boundary of 'D' is at least 10 yards from the goalpost. If a player touches the ball, they're the opposite team gets a penalty.

Further, there are other rules. The second crucial rule is the "offside rule." In this rule; when the player crosses the defender line, it becomes the off-side. If you are a great fan of football, you must know what defenders are

In this sport, the players are into three sub-categories. The first category is "Forward." These are players who put the ball in the goalpost's net. The 2nd category is a "Midfielder."

They pass the ball to the forward player. The 3rd category is the "Defenders." The defenders stop the other team players from putting the ball in the goalpost.

Apart from this, if a player injures and fouls the other team player, the referee gives him a "Yellow" or "Red Card." The yellow card is a warning card, and the red card is a suspension card. This card suspends the play for the rest of the football game.

CHAPTER NINE

MY FAVOURITE PLAYER

MS Dhoni urf Mahendra Singh Dhoni, everyone knows him! He is the shinning superstar of our country. He is the one who makes our country proud of. He is such an expert in cricket that he has fan base of over a millions.

Hard work and reach your goals! Is what's his motive.

Through his entire life and up till now, he has worked so hard to reach the goals in his life. His path is to stay focused. Dedication, hard work, concentration is what all are the steps to success. He is phenomenal! Isn't he? Yah he is!

Mahendra Singh Dhoni was a captain from 11th of September to 4th of January 2017 in limited-overs formats. And in the test series from 2008 to 28th of December 2014. Dhoni holds several numerous captaincy records. He has lead his team towards success.

Padma Shri is the 4rth highest civilian award in the Republic of India. It is given on the basis to the one who has excelled or contributed towards Arts, Education, Industry, Literature, Science, Sports, Medicine, Social Service and Public Affairs.

MS Dhoni achieved this award in the year of 2009.

Rajiv Gandhi Khel Ratna award is the highest sporting honour of the republic of India. This award is named after Rajiv Gandhi, the former prime minister of India who served the nation from 1984 to 1989.

MS Dhoni achieved Rajiv Gandhi Khel Ratna Award in 2007.

the ICC ODI Team of the Year is an honourable award which is given every year by the international cricket council.

MS Dhoni and his team has achieved this honourable award in the year 2013, 2012, 2011, etc

M.S. Dhoni: The Untold Story, which came out in theatres on 30th September 2016.

It touched rs200 crore mark at the box office. The role of MS Dhoni was played by the leading actor Sushant Singh Rajput. He gave complete resemblance of Dhoni in the movie, and gave an excellent performance.

Do you know, that in his bio, it has also been showed that at first Mahendra Singh Dhoni was fond of Football but his coach motivated him for Cricket. It is an amazing movie.

Many people come and go but Dhoni will always remain in our heart, as he is the best player a team could get. There would be more Sachin's and Virat's but there is no one compare to Mahendra Singh Dhoni.

MS Dhoni has few nicknames, his fan base calls him Mahi, or Dhoni.

Dhoni is the shooting star for his parents. His dedication has inspired many. He is the reason behind the Indian team's success.

Outside cricket, Dhoni has a lot of interests in other fields, i.e.,

He has a keen interest towards bikes, which he has oftenly claimed in media. He co-partnered Akkineni Nagarjuna in buying a Supersport World

Championship team Mahi Racing Team India.

And as I have mentioned above that Dhoni had an interest in football so along with Abhishek Bachchan and Vita Dani, Dhoni is now a co-owner of Chennai based Football club Chennaiyin FC, a franchise of the Indian Super League.

Along with Sahara India Pariwar, Dhoni is the co-owner of Ranch Rays.

CHAPTER TEN

MY FAVOURITE FESTIVAL

My favorite holiday is Diwali or Deepavali. It is also called "The Festival of Lights." It is celebrated in October or November by Hindus in India and the Indian Diaspora. It originated more than 2,500 years ago.

Multiple stories are linked to this celebration. One story from northern India tells the story about the great King Rama, one of the avatars of the Hindu god Vishnu. According to the Ramayana, an ancient epic, Rama returned to his kingdom after fourteen years of exile, and defeating the evil demon Ravana, who kidnapped his wife, Sita. On his arrival to Ayodhya, his kingdom, people welcomed him by lighting lamps called diyas. A popular story from southern India is about the Hindu god Krishna, saving sixteen-thousand women from Narakasura, an evil king. In both stories, it is a victory of good over evil. Diwali is also a celebration of goddess Lakshmi.

On the day of Diwali, I like to visit temple, where I pray to Mother Lakshmi. We worship Goddess

Lakshmi for peace, prosperity, and wealth. I also wear new Indian clothes, such as a kurta for men and a sari for women.

We light our homes with diyas, an oil lamp made from clay. We light them by using a cotton wick dipped in ghee or oil. This is one of the reasons that Diwali is called as "The Festival of Lights." This signifies the victory of good over evil and the dispelling of darkness. We also share sweets with our friends and family.

There are many delicious milk sweets, cashew sweets, and almond sweets my family prepares, but out of all of these delectable desserts, my favorite is Gulab Jamun. It is a milk sweet soaked in a sugar syrup.

The most enjoyable part of Diwali for me and my most favorite part of diwali, is lighting sparklers with my family. The magnanimous light of the sparklers and saying "Happy Diwali" to my family helps me find the true spirit of Diwali, which is togetherness. This reminds me of the Fourth of July, because both of them have grand celebrations.

There are so many celebrations around the world like Halloween and Thanksgiving, but my favorite is Diwali.

CHAPTER ELEVEN

MY FAVOURITE PLACE

Paris is the capital city of France and is very popular. It is regarded as the City of Light. It is located on the Seine River which divides the city. Many tourists visit it and have been fascinated towards its status of being one of the most appealing, glamorous, and romantic of all the cities.

My favorite city Paris is a wonderful city where you can see many fascinating things and sights. It is preferred that when you visit there you should opt for a boat tour to get the view of the whole city. You can find the boats on Seine River named Bateaux Mouche. Here you will find day and night rides. If you are riding at night, you will also find dinner here.

The city's great hidden treasure is its own people. Its people are very honest, sincere, warm, and welcoming. This is the thing that inspires the travelers most. And no doubt the sincere behavior of its people is also the reason for liking the city.

There exist superb hotels, cafes, and restaurants where you can eat your favorite food. The high quality of foods and hotels are easily approachable in Paris. The city's popular food includes the appetizer named escargot. A very tasty dessert which you can find here, which is their specialty is Crame Brulee. Moreover, Paris is very famous for making pastries. They offer the best pastries all over the world.

As we know that Paris produced many artists in different fields so it produces photographers also. Its inventor named Nicephore Niepce generated the first everlasting photograph on a refined and smooth pewter shield in Paris in 1825. Moreover, several photographers gained a reputation for their photography in Paris which includes the name of Eugene Atget also. He is well known for his portrayal of street scenes. Other photographers include the names of Robert Doisneau and Marcel Bovis. So Paris has made much progress in this field also.

As we know that Paris produced many artists in different fields so it produces photographers also. Its inventor named Nicephore Niepce generated the first everlasting photograph on a refined and smooth pewter shield in Paris in 1825. Moreover, several photographers gained a reputation for their photography in Paris which includes the name of Eugene Atget also.

CHAPTER TWELVE

MY FAVOURITE CARTOON

"Sometimes, the smallest things take up the most room in your heart."

The cartoon has always been an important part of my lifestyle during childhood. I always used to connect myself with the cartoon characters. It's not only me who loved cartoons this much. There are lots of younger people across the world who love this illustration work. They personally love the fact that cartoons are stress relievers. The cartoon series not only meant to entertain us, but they play a very important role in teaching. We have also seen that nowadays, small kids are learning through cartoon animation. They find it very interesting and entertaining at the same time. I have a long list of my favorite cartoons, but I will share my top favorite cartoon series. Therefore, here are some of my favorite cartoon characters and series.

My Favourite Cartoon is Doraemon

Doraemon is my 2nd favorite cartoon show. He is a cat robot who has superpowers. He lives at nobita's house. Nobita is a very lazy character but innocent. He always gets himself in trouble, and whenever he is in trouble, Doraemon will be there to help him. Nobita has a female friend named Shizuka. Nobita has several enemies, too, Suniyo and Jian. They are best friends but still bully nobita. They always put nobita in trouble and make him feel embarrassed in front of Shizuka. But Doraemon always comes to help him. By using his superpower and gadgets, he teaches a lesson to suniyo and Jian.

Also, Jian is a very bad singer. He always irritates people by singing songs. Doraemon loves nobita and Doraemon always helps nobita in his homework. After all, they are cartoon characters and we need to see them for entertainment purposes only. Doraemon teaches lots of positive lessons like Nobita to have Doraemon, but we don't. So we should not wait for Doraemon to come and help us. We should do it by ourselves. Another lesson which the show Doraemon teaches is that we should not bully someone. These are the reasons why I love Doraemon. I am sure that many younger generation kids love this show.

CHAPTER THIRTEEN

MY FAVOURITE FREEDOM FIGHTERS

India has seen a lot of freedom fighters fight for their motherland. While I respect each and every one of them equally, I have a few personal favorites who inspired me to work for my country. Firstly, I completely adore the father of the nation, Mahatma Gandhi. I like him because he chose the path of non-violence and won freedom without any weapons, only the truth and peace.

Secondly, Rani Lakshmi Bai was a great freedom fighter. I have learned so many things from this empowering woman. She fought for the country despite so many hardships. A mother never gave up her country because of her child, instead took him to the battlefield to fight against injustice. Moreover, she was so inspiring in numerous ways.

Next, Netaji Subhash Chandra Bose comes in my list. He led the Indian National Army to show the power of India to the British. His famous line remains to be 'give me your blood and I will give you freedom.'

Finally, Pandit Jawaharlal Nehru was also one of the greatest leaders. Despite being from a rich family, he gave up the easy life and fought for India's freedom. He was imprisoned a number of times but that did not stop him from fighting against injustice. He was a great inspiration to many.

In short, freedom fighters are what made our country what it is today. However, we see nowadays people are fighting for everything they stood against. We must come together to not let communal hatred come between and live up to the Indian dream of these freedom fighters. Only then will we honor their sacrifices and memory.

CHAPTER FOURTEEN

MY FAVOURITE SUBJECT

Personally, my favorite subject is English. I have always scored well on the subject because I understand it well. It makes learning effortless and I always manage to get good marks. There are other subjects I like too but English definitely tops my list. I never get bored of it and am always ready to study it.

There are many reasons as to why I enjoy studying English. The major one is that it enhances my reading skills. Ever since my childhood, my mother has always read stories to me. So, I developed a habit of reading and listening to stories. As my reading skills get polished through English, it helps me in other subjects too. I grasp the concepts better through reading.

Furthermore, through English, I developed a knack for writing. I absolutely enjoy writing essays and articles. It is only through English, that I started writing my own work. This helps me in forming incredible answers for other subjects as well. It gives me the experience to use accurate words and sentences to convey my message better.

Most importantly, I love fictional stories in English. I love how it always has some lessons in them to learn. They also apply in real life and help me make wise decisions. The stories in English novels and plays always keeps me entertained. It also enhances my imagination powers.

English is definitely a scoring subject which makes it even more special for me. I am an average student who does not take much interest in Science. I manage to get decent marks in the subjects, but in English, I score well. When we compare English to other subjects, we see it is most scoring.

English does not demand word to word answers. It gives the child a chance to play with words. It gives them the creative liberty to speak their minds out. For instance, in Maths, you cannot create your own formulas. You must copy the same exact one taught in the syllabus. But, in English, we can compose our own answers based on our understanding and intelligence.

In addition, English teachers are usually more approachable and understanding. In other subjects, the teachers always have to stick by the book and literally make students mug up the formulas and theories. The English teacher takes time to make them understand each phrase. They allow the students to interpret it as per their intellect. This empowers the child too so they can put their own thinking in it.

In short, I absolutely love English. It gives me the chance to excel without putting too much pressure on me. I get to play with words and form my own interpretations. This helps me get the creative freedom I do not get in other subjects.

CHAPTER FIFTEEN

MY FAVOURITE SEASON

I like the summer season the most. What's not to like about it? You get to enjoy long holidays as everyone gets a break from school. Similarly, parents allow the kids to have ice creams.

Cold drinks are another reasons why summer is my favourite season. We get to have such a wide variety of food items during this season. On the healthier side, we also get incredible mangoes in the summer season.

As mangoes are my favourite fruit, I tend to like summers even more. Summers make us truly appreciate and savour a lot of things. During the summer season, we get holidays for a long time.

During the summer holidays, I get to spend time with my family and friends to the fullest. When we get lucky, we even go on family trips. I look forward to them every year, even if it is a small trip.

Most importantly, there are so many activities that I get to do during summers like joining summer camps, cycling, swimming, and more. Summers are so bright and exciting that it has always been my favourite season.

The Specialty of Summer Season

The summer season has long days and short nights. The days are sunny and bright. We get to relax completely during the afternoons during summers. Similarly, we also get so much sunlight.

The water parks are always full of people during summers that help people stay cool and have a good time. I like swimming in the pools during summers as it makes me feel free. There are also different varieties of food items I get to enjoy during summers.

There are fresh cucumbers, huge watermelons, juicy oranges, sweet guavas, nutritious muskmelons, and more. The early mornings of summer are incredible and nothing can match the atmosphere.

Another speciality of summer has to be the clothes. People enjoy wearing shorts, dresses, sleeveless shirts, and more to enjoy summers to the fullest. The hill stations are swarmed during the summer season as everyone goes there to escape the heat. Therefore, all these specialities make me love summer even more.

All in all, summer is my favourite season as everything is bright and lovely. Even the fruits and vegetables we get are so colourful that it makes a good sight for sore eyes. School going children love summers even more as summer break allows us to play more and relax. Summers are warm, sunny, and delightful.

CHAPTER SIXTEEN

MY FAVOURITE BOOK

"Wings Of Fire" is an auto biography of former President of India and an eminent scientist Shri A.P.J.Abdul Kalam. It is very important for every indian and specially for youth to read this autobiography. It is not because he is a former President and an eminent scientist, therefore every indian should read it, however this autobiography really has good knowledge to share with us, a knowledge which is very difficult to get elsewhere.

This auto biography is different in many ways as it tell us many lessons with true examples. This book tell us a story of a musilm boy, who became the President of a hindu dominated country by hard work and dedication. It gives us an inside look into the lives of Muslims in India and relationship between Hindu and Muslim communities in India. It tells us, how common Hindu and Muslim respect each other's religion.

Wings of Fire is the story of a small boy achieving his dreams despite all the odds. This real story tell us the roll of family,relatives and friends in helping a person

in achieving his goals. This book tell us how to live for our country. This book shows the determination of India and his scientist in achieving excellence in space and missile technology.

This book provides an inside look into the success and failures of indian space and missile technology programs. This Book gives a good presentation about the role of other eminent scientist in shaping our country's future .This book is a must for every student, because this book has the power to motivate a person to excel in life. Wings of Fire is a clear example of achieving one's goals, while fulfilling the commitment towards the country.

CHAPTER SEVENTEEN

MY FAVOURITE ANIMAL

Unlike humans, animals respond with all their love and affection. They would never harm us with malicious intentions. Regardless of its birds or animals, pets have a special bond with their masters.

But when one asks me which is my most favourite animal in this world—a dog always comes to my mind first. Dogs wrap a blanket of security and love for humans. Many adopt dogs because of their wealthy lifestyle, some to increase their home's security. However, many do it for their unconditional love for these furry friends.

One of the features that make me love dogs is their loyalty towards their master or companion. I still remember the day that my father adopted a dog into our family of four. My dog, Zozo, is now our 5th family member. A dog's loyalty is unprecedented.

Most dogs have a very soft fleece of fur, and, it makes it so comforting to pet their soft body. They share their warmth with us emotionally and physically as they are one of the most affectionate among all the domestic animals.

I like to have fun and play with my dog. I usually go on regular walks with him, and whenever I am sad, he sits by my side, and that comforts me with his cute antiques. I feel dogs understand human emotions better than some humans themselves.

Dogs have a great sense of love, but they are way more than some cuddly buddy. Dogs are super smart too, with a killer sense of smell and sight and sharp instincts. There are several breeds to these animals, and, all of them have unique features and characteristics.

Some breeds of dogs like German Shepherd, Belgian Malinois, Bloodhound, Dutch Shepherd, and the retriever breeds are trained to be in the police. Investigation Departments keep Dogs as a security agent to find a critical solution to a problem.

Dogs are pretty smart that they catch up the things very quickly. These trained police dogs find and detect things like drugs or search up human body scents with their strong olfactory senses. They also amp up the security of every household.

When we talk about a dog's eating habits, they are all carnivorous and, so they love to eat meat, fish, rice, bread, and a few other eatables.

Few super loved breeds of dog are the Labrador Retrievers, German Shepherds, Golden Retrievers, French Bulldogs, Bulldogs, Beagles, Poodles, Rottweilers, German Shorthaired Pointers, and Yorkshire Terriers.

If you ever decide to adopt or even buy a dog, remember it's a great responsibility. Dogs are super loyal and lovable, so, you ought to love and care for them as much as they love you. Dogs deserve all the love and care from their masters.

CHAPTER EIGHTEEN

MY FAVOURITE FLOWER

Flowers are the most beautiful flower God has created. They are of different shapes, colours, and different sizes. My favourite flowers are Rose and are known as the flower of love. The rose is found all over the world.

Rose is a very beautiful flower. Some call it the 'King of Flower' and some call it as the 'Queen of Flowers.' Roses grow in different colours like red, white, yellow, pink and many more.

Roses have small thorns on their stem to protect themselves. The rose plant grows in the form of shrubs. A rose plant has round and deep coloured leaves. The unique fruit of the rose plant is called rosehip. The petals of the rose are dried and packed so to use them for scent.

The flower, rose is taken as a symbol, of love and compassion. Different colours of roses stand for different human emotions. Red rose is a symbol of love. Yellow rose stands for friendship. A white rose is

the symbol of purity and pink rose is for joy.

It is famous across the world and people use roses to make garlands. They are used to offer as gifts to someone you love and respect. They are used to make different beauty products. The products like rose water rose fresher and rose perfume are made out of a rose.

More than that, Rose perfume is actually made of the rose oil. The items like rose fallooda, and rose sharbat are also produced using rose.

Because of its importance in people's lives and its engagement with their emotions, every year, on 7th of February, Rose Day is celebrated.

CHAPTER NINETEEN

MY FAVOURITE DISH

Pizza is an Italian dish with a round in shape made with a base of wheat dough on which, the toppings of tomato, onion, capsicum, corn, cheese, and chicken is put with contents of spices then baked in the oven at high-temperature and lastly served with chili flakes and oregano or seasonings.

It has a soft crust after it is baked with cheese and has mouth-watering taste savoring your tongue with spongy and different toppings on it. Pizzas are the best to have for lunch or dinner. It is easily available at affordable rates in many of the restaurants and cafes too.

The Italian dish, Pizza became my favorite when for the first time I had a margarita cheese pizza with extra cheese on it. It was a medium-sized pizza with servings for six people each or three people if they ate in pairs. The Pizza was hot and spongy to touch.

Its top layer was swollen and round shaped. I sprinkled chili flakes and oregano for great taste, and after this when I took a slice of pizza, the cheese was melting and gave yummy taste my tongue. With packed Pizza, inside it also had sachets of tomato sauce that I also tried on another slice of Pizza that I took.

Pizza is an easy dish to make at homes too. I had seen many videos on YouTube telling different ways to make Pizza, in which they had toppings of vegetables and corn too. People who are not having oven for baking, use a pressure cooker or a pan for baking their Pizza using various seasonings.

It could be easily ordered in any size like large for a group of friends or family, medium-sized for a small group and small-sized for an individual. They are made either in fresh pan or hand-tossed, whichever way we want we can have it.

There are up to more than 15 varieties of Pizza's made to serve. There are three variations of Pizza that are Stromboli, panzerotti, and calzone.

thats why I LIKE PIZZA

CHAPTER TWENTY

MY FAVOURITE FLOWER

Mango is my favourite fruit of all times. I love eating mangoes because they are sweet and pulpy. My favourite part about eating mangoes is when we eat it with our hands and even though it becomes a mess, it is always worth it.

Moreover, the memories I have with this fruit makes it even more special. During my summer break, we visit my village along with the whole family. Thus, during the hot summer afternoons, my family sits beneath the tree together.

We take out mangoes from a bucket of cold water and sit down to savour them. Looking back at how much fun we used to have makes me extremely happy. Thus, I always get nostalgic when eating mangoes.

As a result, it brings good memories and happiness in my life. I love eating all varieties of mangoes. When we look back at the pre-historic existence of this fruit in India, we find that it has been around for many

centuries.

As a result, a lot of varieties of mangoes are available. For instance, Alphonso, Kesar, Dasheri, Chausa, Badami and more. Thus, whatever the shape and size, I truly relish the king of fruits.

CHAPTER TWENTY-ONE

MY FAVOURITE MOVIE

Director Jagan Shakti and creative director R. Balki would like you to believe that India's historic Mars mission was built on the back of last-minute improvisation and borrowing a few tricks from the kitchen, helped along by the idea of "jugaad" (a Hindi word that refers to the ability to innovate with limited resources).

With the Mangalyaan satellite, built at one-tenth the cost of NASA's Mars mission and launched by the Indian Space Research Organisation (ISRO) in 2013, India became the first country to send a satellite to the red planet in its first attempt.

Inspired by a photograph of saree-clad women scientists of India's space agency cheering and hugging, that went viral after the launch of the mission, the film places its women at the front and center of its story, much like Theodore Melfi's 2016 Hollywood film, "Hidden Figures".

The 133-minute film begins with a scene in a kitchen, with Tara Shinde (Vidya Balan) rushing through her morning chores while her family lazes around. She reminds her son to eat his meals and tells her husband about errands that need to be run before rushing to work.

At first glance, Shinde is your average working mother. Her career, however, is anything but ordinary – she is a project head at ISRO, where she regularly oversees critical space missions. A misjudgment on her part leads to the aborting of an important mission and her boss, Rakesh Dhawan (Akshay Kumar), takes the brunt of the blame.

He is shunted to the dormant Mars project – India's space agency is notoriously short of funds, and none of the top scientists wants to be a part of the stillborn mission. But Tara has other ideas. Struck by inspiration after she watches flatbread being fried, Tara pitches her low-cost Mars mission idea to Rakesh, who in turn takes it to the bosses.

They put together a rag-tag team of scientists – unlikely picks but effective in their roles, much like the cast of the film. A cushion, a poster, an umbrella – just about everything seems to spark a new idea with this team, which also makes good use of the "turn it off and on again" trick as they rush to build their ambitious satellite.

While the film tries to make the complex science that goes into a space mission accessible, it turns gimmicky in its attempts to simplify the process. The dialogue is trite in places and the writers try too hard to stuff the script with tongue-in-cheek references (including a weak pun about NASA and "sarvanasa", the Sansrkit word for disaster). Fortunately for the film, most of its shortcomings are overshadowed by the camaraderie shared by the cast.

As the childlike scientist who deals with her cranky husband, her rebellious son, and a million-dollar satellite launch with the same equanimity, Vidya Balan is a joy to watch on screen. The performances of Sonakshi Sinha, as an ambitious scientist who reluctantly finds her feet in the program, and Kriti Kulhari, as the quiet divorcee struggling to heal, stand out. Kumar, accustomed to the limelight in most of his films, only pretends to give it up to the women in this film, quickly taking center-stage again when there is a rousing line or two than needs to be delivered.

For all its flaws, "Mission Mangal" is an uplifting film. The film's enthusiasm about its subject and its ability to make you care about its characters help even out the bumps in its path.

CHAPTER TWENTY-TWO

MY STATE

Maharashtra is one of the state of India. It is located in the western part of India. Mumbai is the capital of Maharashtra, and it is also known as the financial capital of India.

There are many reasons to love Maharashtra. Maharashtra is 3rd most significant state in India is wise. It is the second most populated state following Uttar Pradesh if we talk about it population-wise.

Maharashtra has the Arabian Sea flowing on its western coast. The neighboring states of Maharashtra are Gujarat, Madhya Pradesh, Chhattisgarh, Goa, and Karnataka.

The main rivers of Maharashtra are Godavari and Krishna. This state has many big cities like Mumbai, Pune, Aurangabad, Nasik, Nagpur, etc.

As we all know that Maharashtra is a very populated state. There are various types of community living there, such as Hindu, Muslims, Christian, Jain, Buddhist, Sikh, etc.

People of Maharashtra are multi-lingual. They speak many languages, like Hindi, Gujarati, English, Marathi, Kannada, etc.

Places to visit in Maharashtra

Maharashtra has a huge number of places to visit. The Mumbai city is the center of the attraction itself. There are various places to visit in Maharashtra, along with Mumbai. These places include:-

Gateway of India: People who come to Mumbai cannot say no to this place. It is a landmark of Maharashtra. It was built in early 1924.

The local trains of Mumbai are famous across the country as well as all over the world. The very famous railway station of Mumbai is Chhatrapati Shivaji Terminus. It is also famous as CST. This railway station is famous for its extraordinary architectural style. Many Bollywood movies have been shot here.

The ancient temple of Ellora has many stories to tell you. It is a very famous place near Aurangabad.

Ajanta and Ellora caves are declared heritage sites by UNESCO. We can find a hundred caves. Every cave is telling its own story. It has a large number of carvings.

The other ancient caves are Kanheri Caves. It contains Buddhist paintings, and they belong to the 19th century.

Siddhivinayak Temple is a very famous temple of Lord Ganesha. It is located in Mumbai and famous among the devotees across the country.

The Haji Ali dargah is also located in Mumbai.

The Pratapgarh also has its history of the battle. It was won in the 17th century.

The Kolhapur, located very well known as the Mahalakshmi temple, is famous for its architectural styles. It was built in the 12th century. The devotees across the country come here to devote the goddess.

In Maharashtra, there is also an animal sanctuary called The Rajiv Gandhi national park. This place is the house of many animals and birds. The snake park

is the main attraction of this place.

In the Buldhana district of Maharashtra, there is a less known saline water lake with a significant history in Lonar.

There are lots of places in Maharashtra to visit, such as Juhu Chopati in Mumbai, Film city, Taj Palace Hotel, The Krishna temple in Pandharapur.

Famous People of Maharashtra

Maharashtra has always been a land of warriors. When we see the history of Maharashtra, we cannot ignore the famous personalities of Maharashtra, which had a significant role in the foundation of Maharashtra.

Chhatrapati Shivaji is a very famous warrior and idol of Marathas. Marathas worship him. They consider Chhatrapati Shivaji as the leader who established and brought fame to the Maratha Empire when he was ruling.

The most essential personality who is responsible for making the constitution of India, the person who fought for the backward communities, Dr. Baba Saheb Ambedkar was also from Maharashtra.

In the sports industry, there are huge names, which belong to Maharashtra, such as Sachin Tendulkar. People call him God of cricket. He belongs to Mumbai.

Rohit Sharma, Ravi Shashtri, Vinod Kambli, Ajinkya Rahane, etc. are the massive names in the game of cricket. They all belong to Maharashtra.

The film industry of India, which is also famous as Bollywood established in Mumbai. Many film stars are from here.

Sant Tukaram and Namdev are the religious leaders of Maharashtra and fought against the orthodox mentality in society. They were from Maharashtra too.

In the field of politics, Bal Gangadhar Tilak, Bala Saheb Thackrey, Pramod Mahajan, Sharad Pawar, etc. are from Maharashtra.

CHAPTER TWENTY-THREE

MY COUNTRY

India is my homeland. It is the motherland of my ancestors. It is found in South Asia. It is a massive country. It is a country with a population of 100 million people. It is the birthplace of Shiva and Krishna, as well as Buddha and Mahatma Gandhi.

My country is the world's largest democracy. It is home to the world's oldest civilization. It is a prosperous country. It has several natural resources, such as forests, mines, rivers, animals, and so on.

My country has natural frontiers on all sides, thanks to the oceans on three sides and the tremendous Himalayas in the north. India is a secular country where many religions can flourish without being hindered.

My first and foremost thinking is of India. My motherland, India, is one of my favorite places on the planet. India is a country where people of many castes, creeds, faiths, and civilizations coexist and speak a variety of languages.

Spirituality, philosophy, science, and technology are all well-known in India. In India, people of diverse religions such as Hindus, Muslims, Jain, Sikhs, Buddha, and Christians coexist in every corner of the nation. It is also known for farming and agriculture, which is the country's backbone; it employs locally produced food grains and other products. India is also well-known for its tourist attractions since the country's natural beauty draws visitors from all over the world.

Our culture has been passed down through the generations. In the midst of multiplicity, there is a sense of unity. We speak a variety of languages and worship a variety of gods, yet we all share the same spirit. India's soul runs through the land, tying us all together. There are numerous tourist attractions in India.

The Taj Mahal, Fatehpur Sikri, the Qutub Minar, the Red Fort, and the Gateway of India are some of the most famous landmarks in India. The Hawai Mahal, Chandigarh's Rock Garden, Chittorgarh, and Mysore are just a few of the many treasures that draw visitors from all over the world.

Kashmir is abundant in natural beauty. Kashmir has been referred to as "heaven on Earth." The land of valleys, rivers, lakes, and mountains is appropriate for gods to live in.

The sites to visit include Ooty, the Nilgiris Hills, Shimla, and the temples of South India, as well as the Khajuraho Ajanta and Ellora caves. It's the place of my fantasies. My country means a lot to me.

India is home to wonders such as the Taj Mahal, Fatehpur Sikri, the Golden Temple, Qutab Minar, Red Fort, Ooty, Nilgiris, Kashmir, Khajuraho, Ajanta, and Ellora caves. Great rivers, mountains, valleys, lakes, and oceans abound in this country.

It is a Peninsula Island, meaning it is bordered on three sides by oceans: the Bay of Bengal to the east, the Arabian Sea to the west, and the Indian Ocean to the south. The tiger is India's national animal, the peacock is its national bird, the lotus is its national flower, and the mango is its national fruit.

India is a country with a long history of great leaders and independent warriors. Indian soldiers are stationed at the borders to protect our country from terrorists. Great leaders such as Chhatrapati Shivaji, Mahatma Gandhi, Jawaharlal Nehru, Dr. Babasaheb Ambedkar, and great scientists such as Dr. Jagadeesh Chandra Bose, Dr. Homi Bhabha, Dr. C.V Raman, Dr. Naralikar, and great reformers such as Dr. Jagadeesh Chandra Bose, Dr. Homi Bhabha, etc.

It is a secular state in which we live. The delighted followers of the world's numerous religions breathe in her lap. We have a distinct culture that has evolved over time.

The people of India are incredibly diverse. We speak different languages, worship different gods, yet we all have the same Indian spirit that runs through our land, tying us together. We have a tremendous deal of unity in our diversity, and we are the only country in the world where diversity coexists with strong unity and harmony.

India is the world's seventh-largest country by land area, and it is situated in South Asia. From every angle, our country is surrounded by beauty. Bharat and Hindustan are two more names for India, and Indians are the people who live there. Our country's national anthem is "Jan Gan Man," and our country's national song is "Sare Jahan Se Achcha."

India is a democratic country where citizens elect their leaders and live in freedom, meaning they are free to do whatever they choose within the confines of the law. If an Indian citizen tries to injure another person, there are rules and regulations in place to punish him and make him realize his error.

Our country is also amazing due to its stunning mountains, lakes, forests, seas, and oceans, among other things. Many foreign visitors come to India each

year to see the country's natural beauty, which includes its rich historical temples, traditions, language, and heritage, among other things.

CHAPTER TWENTY-FOUR

MUMBAI A DREAM LAND

Mumbai is infectious. Once you start living in Mumbai... I don't think you can live anywhere else."

Mumbai is situated in the west part of India, also called the Financial Capital of India. It is one of the largest cities of India. Mumbai is one of those places in India where the past meets the present. Marathi is considered to be the regional language of Mumbai, as it is a part of Maharashtra. It is also one of the highest populated cities of India. It was also named as the Alpha World City in the year 2008. Interestingly, this city has the most numbers of Millionaires and Billionaires of the country.

Geographical Features of Mumbai

Mumbai, the capital city of Maharashtra, with an area of 603 squared-kilometers, lies on the western coast of India. It made from the group of seven islands, and hence, it is sometimes also called the Island city. These seven islands are as follows: Isle of Bombay,

Mazagaon, Colaba, Old Woman's Island, Parel, Worli, and Salsette Island.

History of Mumbai City

Mumbai was named after a local goddess, Mumba Devi in 1995. The history of this spectacular and modern city dates back to the rule of the famous King Ashoka. These seven islands were under the rule of him until his demise. After his demise, it was ruled by various rulers. And finally, these isles were handed over to the East India Company by the Portuguese in 1668, and then it was named "Bombay".

These islands were finally merged into a single mass through various infrastructure projects in 1845; But it was the opening of the Suez Canal in 1869, that opened the city to the rest of the World. And from here on, Mumbai went on to become a major port in India. Post-Independence, Mumbai went on to become one of the most developed cities of the country, and in 1960, it was declared as the new Capital of Maharashtra.

Places to visit in Mumbai

Gateway of India

The Gateway of India, also known as the Taj Mahal of Mumbai, is located on the waterfront at Apollo Bunder area at the end of Chhatrapati Shivaji Marg, South Mumbai. It was built during the British Raj, to be used as a ceremonial entrance to India for the Viceroys and Governors of Bombay. The structure is 85 feet high.

Marine Drive

Officially named as the Netaji Subhash Chandra Bose Road, it is a 3 km long road along the coastline in southern Mumbai. Large crowds of people gather here, to experience this beautiful walkway and the stunning scenario of the setting sun at dusk. Interestingly, Marine Drive is also known as 'Queen's Necklace', due to the effect of the streetlights surrounding the place, making it appear like pearls when viewed from the top.

Juhu Beach

Also known as the Celebrity Beach of Mumbai, it is one of the most famous and most-visited beaches of India. Tourists visit this beach to experience its peaceful atmosphere and its scenic beauty. Not just that, the beach is also famous for its local street foods.

Elephanta Caves

Located just 10 kilometers away from the mainland Mumbai, the Elephanta Islands consists some of the most artistic caves, i.e. the Elephanta Caves. These caves which were built between around 5th and 8th century. Till then, the caves had survived every calamity that met with it.

Bandra Worli Sea link

Also known as the Rajiv Gandhi Sea Link, it is a cable bridge that connects Bandra to Worli. This bridge stands as an example of one of the brilliant engineering miracles. The length of this bridge is around 5.6 kilometres and had decreased the traffic by a considerable amount. And many more places are there to visit.

CHAPTER TWENTY-FIVE

EDUCATION

Education is the most significant tool in eliminating poverty and unemployment. Moreover, it enhances the commercial scenario and benefits the country overall. So, the higher the level of education in a country, the better the chances of development are.

In addition, this education also benefits an individual in various ways. It helps a person take a better and informed decision with the use of their knowledge. This increases the success rate of a person in life.

Subsequently, education is also responsible for providing with an enhanced lifestyle. It gives you career opportunities that can increase your quality of life.

Similarly, education also helps in making a person independent. When one is educated enough, they won't have to depend on anyone else for their livelihood. They will be self-sufficient to earn for themselves and lead a good life.

Above all, education also enhances the self-confidence of a person and makes them certain of things in life. When we talk from the countries viewpoint, even then education plays a significant role. Educated people vote for the better candidate of the country. This ensures the development and growth of a nation.

Get the huge list of more than 500 Essay Topics and Ideas

Doorway to Success

To say that education is your doorway to success would be an understatement. It serves as the key which will unlock numerous doors that will lead to success. This will, in turn, help you build a better life for yourself.

An educated person has a lot of job opportunities waiting for them on the other side of the door. They can choose from a variety of options and not be obligated to do something they dislike. Most importantly, education impacts our perception

positively. It helps us choose the right path and look at things from various viewpoints rather than just one.

With education, you can enhance your productivity and complete a task better in comparison to an uneducated person. However, one must always ensure that education solely does not ensure success.

It is a doorway to success which requires hard work, dedication and more after which can you open it successfully. All of these things together will make you successful in life.

In conclusion, education makes you a better person and teaches you various skills. It enhances your intellect and the ability to make rational decisions. It enhances the individual growth of a person.

Education also improves the economic growth of a country. Above all, it aids in building a better society for the citizens of a country. It helps to destroy the darkness of ignorance and bring light to the world.

CHAPTER TWENTY-SIX

MY HOBBY

Our lives daily is a constant race with time. However, sometimes life spares us with an ample amount of time for ourselves, and it is up to an individual how well he utilizes his leisure time. Different people pursue different activities for engaging themselves and getting rid of boredom. For me, it has always been dancing to the tunes of my favorite songs. I have always been an introvert, shy at nature, a person of few words, and for someone like me, dance is the best form of expression of the body, mind, and soul. When your feet tap to the beats of extravagant music and your hands match the rhythms of your soul, dance is born and it adds years to your life.

To be honest, it is tough to explain dance in words because I feel dance is a language in itself that speaks for all cultures and traditions. It's the common thread that binds the beads of various communities, regions and brings the world together. It provides easy access for exploring the best of all beautiful cultures. Different forms of dance involve different emotions. Some are prehistoric. A few give insights into the diverse traditions prevalent in society. You can learn a lot about one's country through the form of dance portrayed by their artists.

Dance has always been fascinating to me for the very reason of its taste in diversity and integrity, how people from all over the world can connect themselves and communicate with each other through dance. Some native dance forms talk about the king's, the rulers, the invaders and many of the historical times. Others are a way of celebration of different festivals. I have tried to pick up a few of my favorite dance forms that drew my attention.

Contemporary Dance:

Just like yoga, contemporary form of dance bridges the gap between our body and mind and establishes a soulful connection. Controlling the movements of our legs forms the crucial part of this dance. It is typically done barefooted, this form allows creativity to be the captain of the ship.

Ballet Dance:

As we know, dance is the simplest form of expression have you ever wondered how a dance form could narrate a story. I am talking about ballet, the famous type of dance. It can be done by sheer practice, dedication and techniques. The ballet dancers often wear slippers and pointe shoes for adding grace to this form. To add soul, it is categorically performed on classical songs.

Tap Dance:

This dance form is an option for the people who have ever had a fetish for shoes. It is typically performed by artists wearing a specially designed shoe having soles made out of metal plates to create a tapping sound, justifying the origin of the dance name. Although the upper bodies and arms are involved, it is a matter of pure footjob.

Jazz Dance:

For all the people with their energy flowing out in unknown directions, this dance form is for them. Jazz is a type of dance that requires a tremendous amount of power and strength. Your personalities can be beautifully portrayed in this form. Performed on upbeat music, it is the right way of channelizing all your extra energies productively. You have to get that swiftness to match its superfast beats, or you will miss a step in the blink of the eye.

Hip-hop Dance:

Well, coming to hip-hop, it is similar to the energies required in jazz, but it also allows freedom to the dancer to add bits of his personality traits. Originating from the famous hip-hop culture, this dance form has given rooms to popping, locking and crumping as well.

Ballroom Dance:

The type of romance, love and sparks between a man and a woman is what ballroom talks about. It is an engagement of two partners and their social affair. Cha cha, samba, tango, Paso doble, waltz are definitely some of the most popular ballroom types.

A hobby is undoubtedly a means to pass the free time, but what if it also has a productive impact on your health and lifestyle. Dancing is the type of activity that not only strengthens your body but also tames your mind. Your muscles get toned and your body stays fit and fine. A healthy body is a must for healthy survival and in today's world, the awareness for health has tremendously increased. People are conscious of how they look and how well their bodies can cope up with the changing lifestyles. Dancing apart from providing overall increased muscular strength also helps in building strong bones, thus preventing osteoporosis, which is common after a certain age. It sharpens one's motors and provides improved functioning of the heart and lungs. It's a great coordinator between the mind and body, thereby balancing the emotional and psychological needs. Obesity, which is generally a significant issue, can also be overcome by rigorous dancing, thus helping in efficient weight management. When you look good, you think right, and your confidence boosts up to a completely new level.

Why I choose dancing as my hobby?

Having addressed all the fundamental aspects of dancing, I would come back to my hobby dancing, why I chose to be associated with it and how much I am into it. Growing up as the only child in the family, I was bored most of the time, and since there was nobody around, my parents sent me to a dance class. I was not very sure if I would actually like spending time on dancing to some hit melodies, but no sooner, I joined the class, my perspective towards dancing changed, for the better. I started taking a keen interest in the steps taught, and I would practice them for hours in my room until I earned perfection. I would go wrong many times, but my dance teacher Lily Ma'am would always be there like my guiding angel correcting all my postures and constantly reminding me of the following steps. I could actually feel the vibes from my fellow dance mates and the kind of confidence I was building made my parents and me very happy. I could sense a rise in my self-esteem and I was no longer the under confident shy kid. I would participate in many dance events and perform gracefully. My teachers would also be proud of me and encourage me to the fullest.

CHAPTER TWENTY-SEVEN

MY AMBITION

My ambition is to become an IAS officer. Though I know that the magnitude of civil services exam is tough but still I feel it is a challenge to relish upon. IAS – Indian Administrative Service sounds and preludes a sense of pride in the minds of the selected candidates. To lead a district/bunch of villages is not a simple joke and every time you need to be on your toes, manage crisis and you need to be a decision maker as well as an efficient leader.The very wish of me becoming an IAS officer is infused by the social evils that prevail in the society. The sufferings faced by poor and the destitute ignite the spirit in one's self and instigate the proceedings. Every one should at least have access to basic amenities like food, shelter, clothing etc. Nothing can be changed in a day's time, but it is possible only by the cumulative efforts of all people. If India is to become a super-power, she needs to get out of the webs of poverty, unemployment, social inequality and communal riots. So why IAS?? I don't want to myself lie between the cobwebs of matrimony and job. Indeed I want to contribute something for the nation for her progress and development. India is in urgent need of youths who are determined for the sake of the nation. IAS officer to some extent can

spur a change in the lives of people under his control. The task doesn't end here and one needs to devote his soul to the nation building politics. The infusion of young blood in politics will surely have a great impact in the development of our nation. Ambition affords no greater responsibility, no greater privilege than the raising of the next generation.

CHAPTER TWENTY-EIGHT

MY INSPIRATION

There are many people that have had an impact on my life and influenced me in many different ways. My mother, however, has had the biggest impact on my life, and influenced me more than anyone else. She has had an impact on me since the day I was born, and she still does today. Before I could even talk, I am sure she had an impact on me by the way she took care of me as an infant. My mother has always been a Christian. That has influenced me throughout my whole life. Even though my mother did not see it, she did have an influence on me throughout my high school years also. As a baby, my mother had an impact on me. I was little, but I know she still did. When I would cry, she would come and see what I needed. She would change my diaper if it needed changed, or she would feed me if that is what I wanted. If there was something else wrong with me, she would definitely find it out. She would not stop trying until I stopped crying. If my mother had left me in my crib crying for hours, I would have realized soon that she probably did not really care about me. When I got a little older,

It was just 3 a.m. and the sky was still in the darkness of an extremely cold evening winter in the severe highland. The wind blew fast made the dark sky become more dangerous and violent, but my mother was ready to set out again. Hardly did anyone know that where a female was going in such that weather. She was going to remote areas of the province to do her business, retailing commodities. At the age of 40s, my mother still had to work hard to earn her living and support our family. By her old bike with a lot of goods that maybe was out of her ultimate limit, my mother faced her new challenge alone but vigorously. There was no light outside, no stars, and no one, there was only winds still blew faster and faster towards my mother's sunburnt face. This moment of my mother' life that has been instilled in my mind has tremendously helped me in my spiritual, mental, and developmental

CHAPTER TWENTY-NINE

MY BEST FRIEND

I have a best friend ever in my life named divya . SHe is someone special in my life who helps me in my every difficulty. SHe is someone who showed me right path. SHe always has time for me even in his busy schedule. SHe is my neighbour that's why we become together even after school time. We go together at picnic whenever we get vacation from school. We enjoy our festival holidays together and with each other's family. We go to see Ramlila fair in the Ramlila ground together and enjoy a lot. We always take part in every extracurricular activities of the school. We love to play cricket and carom at home. He is more than a mentor for me because he always gives me right decisions whenever I become in difficulty.

SHe is so special for me in my life; I never do anything without her. SHe always become in a good mood and never compromise with wrong ways. SHe always does right things and motivates every one of us in the classroom to do the same. SHe always has smiling face even in her difficult times and never let his difficulties to come on his face. SHe is a good counsellor and loves to explain anything. SHe cares for her parents, grandparents and other family members. she obeys them always and other old people of the society. I met her first time when I was in the fifth grade and now we are in 8th standard in the same section.

He is very tall and looks different from my other classmates. Once I was very upset because of money problem. I could not buy all necessary books in the class 6. He asked me, what happened and I told him my story. He said that, for this small problem you are so worry and not happy for some days. He laughed and told me that don't worry we can share all books in the school as well as at home. You don't need to buy even any single book for whole year. After that he made me laugh through his jokes and stories. I never forget that moment he helped me and always become ready to help him too. He is so practical and never mixes the personal and professional life. He helps me always whenever I get difficulties in solving my Maths homework. Our likes and dislikes never match however we are best friends.

CHAPTER THIRTY

MY GARDEN

A Garden is the best place in the house according to me. As it is the only place where a person can get relief from a busy life. Moreover having a garden in the house welcomes many health benefits. For instance, a garden has many plants that give oxygen.

My garden contains different types of plants. For instance, it has different flowers such as roses, sunflowers, Lilies, daisies. These flowers are the easiest to grow and flourish the environment with their beautiful smells. Moreover, the colors of these flowers make a garden look beautiful.

Further, my garden has different vegetables growing in them. For example vegetables like tomato, carrots, sweet potato, cauliflower, bell pepper, etc. These are the easiest to grow. Apart from this, they have various health benefits. Furthermore, this ensures that the vegetables are fresh and free from any chemicals.

The garden has grass all over the area. As a result, this makes it the best place for any exercise. Furthermore, it has a soft ground where children can play different sports.

This ensures that they do not get hurt even if they fall down while playing. Further, my garden has a swing too which is my favorite. Because I can spend hours swinging on it and do not get bored. Sometimes I spend my entire day in the garden completing all my tasks there. But this is only possible whenever I have a holiday.

CHAPTER THIRTY-ONE

MY PLANET

The rocks make up the earth that has been around for billions of years. Similarly, water also makes up the earth. In fact, water covers 70% of the surface. It includes the oceans that you see, the rivers, the sea and more.

Thus, the remaining 30% is covered with land. The earth moves around the sun in an orbit and takes around 364 days plus 6 hours to complete one round around it. Thus, we refer to it as a year.

Just like revolution, the earth also rotates on its axis within 24 hours that we refer to as a solar day. When rotation is happening, some of the places on the planet face the sun while the others hide from it.

As a result, we get day and night. There are three layers on the earth which we know as the core, mantle and crust. The core is the centre of the earth that is usually very hot. Further, we have the crust that is the outer layer. Finally, between the core and crust, we have the mantle i.e. the middle part.

The layer that we live on is the outer one with the rocks. Earth is home to not just humans but millions of other plants and species. The water and air on the earth make it possible for life to sustain. As the earth is the only livable planet, we must protect it at all costs.

There is No Planet B

The human impact on the planet earth is very dangerous. Through this essay on earth, we wish to make people aware of protecting the earth. There is no balance with nature as human activities are hampering the earth.

Needless to say, we are responsible for the climate crisis that is happening right now. Climate change is getting worse and we need to start getting serious about it. It has a direct impact on our food, air, education, water, and more.

The rising temperature and natural disasters are clear warning signs. Therefore, we need to come together to save the earth and leave a better planet for our future generations.

Being ignorant is not an option anymore. We must spread awareness about the crisis and take preventive measures to protect the earth. We must all plant more trees and avoid using non-biodegradable products.

Further, it is vital to choose sustainable options and use reusable alternatives. We must save the earth to save our future. There is no Planet B and we must start acting like it accordingly.

CHAPTER THIRTY-TWO

MAHATMA GANDHI

Mohandas Karamchand Gandhi, who was also known as Mahatma, "Great Soul" Gandhi, was a hero, as well as a political and spiritual leader of India. He was of the Hindu faith, of which I am too. Mohandas brought India to independence by using non-violent resistance. He thought that there was injustice being served to the Indians, especially to the immigrants by the South Africans. Gandhi was born on October 2, 1869 in Porbandar, Kathiawar, now known as Gujarat. Gandhi passed away at the age of 78 on January 30, 1948. Mahatma Gandhi was brought up in India near Rajkot, where he did most of his studies. In 1888, Gandhi went to London, leaving his wife and son behind, to pursue his degree in law. Later in 1893, Gandhi went to South Africa to work and found that there was a lot of prejudice towards Indians. That was the reason Gandhi began protesting and eventually he became an inspiring hero for millions. The three main qualities that define Gandhi as a hero are his strong leadership, simplicity and bravery.

Leadership was one of Gandhi's heroic qualities. One way he demonstrated leadership was by encouraging people in his village to start using homespun clothing. Homespun was one of Gandhi's favorite hobbies. Introducing homespun to his village promised the growth of the village's economy. The poor became employed to make homespun clothes for others in the village and outside of their own village. This drastically diminished the poverty in Gandhi's village. Moreover, Gandhi ended the issue of discrimination against untouchables. Back in those days, the Hindus used to discriminate against the untouchables, who were their own kind but just low in the caste system. The untouchables are just another word to describe poor, less educated people who really didn't fit in with the middle class people. Gandhi made the Hindus realize that what British people were doing to them is the same thing that they were doing to the untouchables. This made the Hindus realize what they were doing to the untouchables. Last but not least, the Indian Independence Movement was the all-time heroic deed led by Gandhi. This movement was accomplished in 1947 by Mahatma. This movement took place because India was governed by the British, and Gandhi wanted India to become independent. Therefore, Gandhi showcased many outstanding leadership skills that made him a hero

Simplicity is the second most heroic quality that Gandhi demonstrated. Gandhi believed in living a simple life. He wanted a simple life, with only the necessities that he needed. Even though he was a barrister (a lawyer), he had no arrogance. He dressed like a poor person and he only wore clothes that were homespun, made out of khadi (cotton). He was a vegetarian and then became a fruitarian; many days he would go without eating and would not complain. He was also a man of truth because everything he did and said, he did it with truth. Because he believed in truth, he wrote a book titled, The Story of My Experiments with Truth. Moreover, even though he did many heroic things, he claimed to be an average man: "I claim to be no more than an average man with less than average ability" . This quote tells the readers that he did not want to be known as Gandhi, he did not want everyone worshiping him, and he was just proving that he is an average person like others. In addition, what made him a hero can make anyone a hero, only if they have the will to do the right thing and if they believe in truth, nonviolence and creating peace among others. As a result, Gandhi believed that simplicity and truth can make anyone a hero.

Bravery is another quality that describes Gandhi. Gandhi did many big things that show how brave he was. The first example of his brave work was the Dandi March. The Dandi March was an Indian march led by Gandhi for salt. This was the first act of opposition towards the British and the beginning of the movement to get India's independence. Gandhi broke the Salt Law made by the British and was imprisoned for many years. The Dandi March, with more than enough Indians and with the support of Gandhi, diminished the Salt Tax that people had to pay. Gandhi was also very brave to fight for his country on his own and also to sacrifice himself. Many times he got beaten up by the British people, but he did not say one word. He did not execute any type of violent behavior towards them. This is because he was a strong believer in nonviolence. Lastly, Gandhi

showed bravery by doing what he believed was right. He believed that things can be done with love and not war, which definitely results in peace. He believed in his own principles for many years till he died, and he fought for India believing that the only way to end the hatred and war is through peace and love. For that reason, Gandhi is a true hero to all because of his bravery and what he did for India's independence.

CHAPTER THIRTY-THREE

APJ ABDUL KALAM

APJ Abdul kalam is a famous name in the whole world. He is counted among the greatest scientists of the 21st century. Even more, he becomes the 11th president of India and served his country. He was the most valued person of the country as his contribution as a scientist and as a president is beyond compare. Apart from that, his contribution to the ISRO (Indian Space Research Organization) is remarkable. He headed many projects that contributed to the society also he was the one who helped in the development of Agni and Prithvi missiles. For his involvement in the Nuclear power in India, he was known as "Missile Man of India". And due to his contribution to the country, the government awarded him with the highest civilian award.

APJ Abdul Kalam was born in Tamil Nadu. At that time the financial condition of his family was poor so from an early age he started supporting his family financially. But he never gave up education. Along with supporting his family he continued his studies and completed graduation. Above all, he was a member of the Pokhran nuclear test conducted in

1998.

There is a countless contribution of Dr.APJ Abdul Kalam to the country but he was most famous for his greatest contribution that is the development of missiles that goes by the name Agni and Prithvi.

The great missile man becomes the President of India in 2002. During his presidency period, the army and country achieved many milestones that contributed a lot to the nation. He served the nation with an open heart that's why he was called 'people's president'. But at the end of his term period, he was not satisfied with his work that's why he wanted to be the President a second time but later on forfeited his name.

After leaving the presidential office at the end of his term Dr. APJ Abdul Kalam again turn to his old passion which is teaching students. He worked for many renowned and prestigious institute of India located across the country. Above all, according to his the youth of the country is very talented but need the opportunity to prove their worth that's why he supported them in their every good deed.

He died during delivering a lecture to students in Shillong by sudden cardiac arrest in 2015. He was an outstanding scientist and a pioneer engineer who served his entire life for the nation and died while serving it. The man had the vision to make India a great country. And according to his the youth are the

real assets of the country that's why we should inspire and motivate them.

CHAPTER THIRTY-FOUR

Dr. BABASAHEB AMBEDKAR

Dr. Baba Saheb Ambedkar was one of the first Dalits to get a complete education in India. He achieved a degree in political science, economics, and law. He was a great lawyer, writer, historian, and also one of the great political leaders. He was born in Madhya Pradesh.

He was born on 14th April 1990, and hence we celebrate this day as the birth anniversary of Dr. Ambedkar – Ambedkar Jayanti. Bhimabai and Ramji Maloji Sakpal were parents of Dr. Ambedkar. He is mostly known as "Baba Saheb". Ambedkar Jayanti is mostly celebrated in Maharashtra by Dalits because he always fought for the rights of Dalits.

He himself has faced a lot of injustice in his life. His education journey was not much easier than others. After independence, Dalits were treated as "untouchable". They were facing a lot of discrimination everywhere. Dr. Baba Saheb

Ambedkar came ahead and fought for them and got Dalits their equal rights and freedom as others.

Dr. Ambedkar contributed a lot to make in Indian Law and Education. Dr. Amdedkar formed a political party which was called as "Independent Labour Party". After India got independence, he was the first minister of law and committee chairman who forms the Indian Constitution.

Dr. Baba Saheb Ambedkar contributed a lot in forming law, order, and constitution of India. He was always against the discrimination happening against the Dalits. He forms new laws in support of Dalits and gave them education and equal rights as other castes.

One of the biggest achievements of Dr. Ambedkar was Bharat Ratna. He won the Bharat Ratna award in 1990. He was a scientist, sociologist, freedom fighter, journalist, human rights activist, philosopher, and much more. Dr. Baba Saheb Ambedkar completed his post-graduate from Columbia University and London School of Economics. Ambedkar is an inspiration of young lawyers across the world.

Dr. Ambedkar was one of the greatest leaders in the history of India. We should pay him respect and tribute on what he has contributed to Indian law and constitution. He helped Dalits and made sure they get what they deserve! Because of him, many students are able to get quality education in India at a lesser fee.

There are people who are economically backward and cannot afford education in the high-level institute, but because Baba Saheb even they are able to get high-quality education for their children which will secure the future of India.

CHAPTER THIRTY-FIVE

LOKMANYA

Bal Gangadhar Tilak was a great freedom fighter and a third of the famous trio Lal Bal Pal, representing Lala Lajpat Rai, Bal Gangadhar Tilak, and Bipin Chandra Pal. Tilak along with two of his contemporaries was involved in Anti-British agitation and the boycott of British goods.

A Courageous Nationalist

Bal Gangadhar Tilak's defiant patriotism and courage set him apart from other political leaders. He openly criticized the oppressive policies of the British, when he was just a teacher in Maharashtra.

He had a penchant for writing and started a newspaper titled 'Kesari', openly supporting revolutionary activities against the British Rule. He had been to prison on several occasions for Anti-British activities and for supporting other revolutionaries.

Sedition charges had been pressed against Bal Gangadhar Tilak by the British government on three occasions – 1897, 1909 and 1916. He had also been imprisoned in Mandalay, Burma for supporting Prafulla Chaki and Khudiram Bose. The duo was convicted in a bomb attack on Muzaffarpur's Chief Presidency Magistrate, Douglas Kingsford, in which two British women were killed. He spent six years from 1908 to 1914 at Mandalay.

Bal Gangadhar Tilak was a great freedom fighter and a third of the famous trio Lal Bal Pal, representing Lala Lajpat Rai, Bal Gangadhar Tilak, and Bipin Chandra Pal. Tilak along with two of his contemporaries was involved in Anti-British agitation and the boycott of British goods.

A Courageous Nationalist

Bal Gangadhar Tilak's defiant patriotism and courage set him apart from other political leaders. He openly criticized the oppressive policies of the British, when he was just a teacher in Maharashtra.

He had a penchant for writing and started a newspaper titled 'Kesari', openly supporting revolutionary activities against the British Rule. He had been to prison on several occasions for Anti-British activities and for supporting other revolutionaries.

Sedition charges had been pressed against Bal Gangadhar Tilak by the British government on three occasions – 1897, 1909 and 1916. He had also been imprisoned in Mandalay, Burma for supporting Prafulla Chaki and Khudiram Bose. The duo was convicted in a bomb attack on Muzaffarpur's Chief Presidency Magistrate, Douglas Kingsford, in which two British women were killed. He spent six years from 1908 to 1914 at Mandalay.

CHAPTER THIRTY-SIX

BHAGAT SINGH

Bhagat Singh was considered to be one of the most famous revolutionaries of the Bharatiya Independence movement. For this reason, he is often referred to as 'Shaheed' (martyr) Bhagat Singh. At such a young age, if anyone was smiling just before being hanged to death, it was Martyr Bhagat Singh. His uncle, Sardar Ajit Singh, as well as his father, were great freedom fighters, so he grew up in a patriotic atmosphere. At an early age, he started dreaming of uprooting the British empire. Never afraid of fighting during his childhood, he thought of 'growing guns in the fields', so that he could fight the British. The Ghadar Movement left a deep imprint on his mind. Kartar Singh Sarabha, hanged at the age of 19, became his hero. The massacre at Jallianwala Bagh on 13th April, 1919 drove him to Amritsar, where he kissed the earth sanctified by the martyrs' blood and brought back home a little of the soaked soil. At the age of 16, he used to wonder why so many Bharatiyas could not drive away a fistful of invaders.

Born: 28th Sept. 1907, Punjab

Died: Hanged in the early hours of 23rd March 1931.

In search of revolutionary groups and ideas, he met Sukhdev and Rajguru. Bhagat Singh, along with the help of Chandrashekhar Azad, formed the Hindustan Socialist Republican Army (HSRA). The aim of this Bharatiya revolutionary movement was now defined as not only to make Bharat independent, but also to create a socialist Bharat.

A brutal attack by the police on veteran freedom fighter Lala Lajpat Rai at an anti-British procession caused his death on 17th November 1928, in Lahore. Bhagat Singh determined to avenge Lajpat Rai's death by shooting the British official responsible for the killing, Deputy Inspector General Scott. He shot down Assistant Superintendent Saunders instead, mistaking him for Scott.

Then he made a dramatic escape from Lahore to Calcutta and from there to Agra, where he established a bomb factory. The British Government responded to the act by imposing severe measures like the Trades Disputes Bill. It was to protest against the passing of the Bill that he threw bombs in the Central Assembly Hall (now our Loksabha) while the Assembly was in session. The bombs did not hurt anyone, but the noise they made was loud enough to wake up an enslaved Nation from a long sleep. After throwing the bombs, Bhagat Singh and his friend deliberately courted arrest by refusing to run away from the scene. During

his trial, Bhagat Singh refused to employ any Defense counsel.

CHAPTER THIRTY-SEVEN

LAL BAHADUR SHASTRI

Since childhood, Lal Bahadur Shastri was very honest and laborious. Lal Bahadur Shastri was graduated with a first-class degree from the Kashi Vidyapeeth in 1926 then he was given the title Shastri Scholar. Lal Bahadur Shastri acquired virtues like boldness, love of adventure, patience, self-control, courtesy, and selflessness in his childhood. In order to participate actively in the freedom movement, Lal Bahadur Shastri compromised even with his studies.

Lal Bahadur Shastri got married to Lalita Devi. And both Lal Bahadur Shastri and his wife blessed with 6 children. The name of their children was Kusum, Hari Krishna, Suman, Anil, Sunil, and Ashok.

Lal Bahadur Shastri was drawn towards the national struggle for freedom when he was a boy. He was very impressed by Gandhi's speech which was delivered on the foundation ceremony of Banaras Hindu University. After that, he became a loyal follower of Gandhi and then after jumped into the freedom movement. Because of this, he had to go to jail many

times. Lal Bahadur Shastri was always believed that self-sustenance and self-reliance as the pillars to build a strong nation. Lal Bahadur Shastri wished to be remembered by his work rather than well-rehearsed speeches proclaiming lofty promises. He was always against the prevailing caste system and therefore decided to drop his surname and after his graduation, he get Shastri surname.

Lal Bahadur Shastri was also known for his simplicity, patriotism, and honesty. India lost a great leader. He had given the talent and integrity to India. His death was still a mystery. Lal Bahadur Shastri had political associations is Indian National Congress. He had the political ideology such as nationalist, liberal, right-wing. Lal Bahadur Shastri is a Hinduism religion. He was always self-sustenance and self-reliance as the pillars to build a strong nation.

CHAPTER THIRTY-EIGHT

SHUBHASH CHANDRA BOSE

Subhash Chandra Bose was a great Indian nationalist. People even today know him by love for his country. This true Indian man was born on the 23rd of January in 1897. Most noteworthy, he fought with bravery against the British rule. Subhash Chandra Bose was certainly a revolutionary freedom fighter.

The participation of Subhash Chandra Bose took place with the Civil Disobedience Movement. This is how Subhash Chandra Bose became part of the Indian Independence movement. He became a member of the Indian National Congress (INC). Also, in 1939 he became the party president. However, this was for a short time only because of his resignation from this post.

The British put Subhash Chandra Bose under house arrest. This was because of his opposition to British rule. However, due to his cleverness, he secretly left the country in 1941. He then went to Europe to seek help against the British. Most noteworthy, he sought the help of Russians and Germans against the British.

Subhash Chandra Bose went to Japan in 1943. This was because the Japanese gave their agreement to his appeal for help. In Japan Subhash Chandra Bose began the formation of the Indian National Army. Most noteworthy, he did the formation of a provisional government. The axis powers during the Second World War certainly recognized this provisional government.

The Indian National Army attacked the North-eastern parts of India. Furthermore, this attack took place under the leadership of Subhash Chandra Bose. Also, the INA was successful in capturing a few portions. Unfortunately, there was the surrender of INA due to weather and Japanese policies. However, Bose made his Refusal to surrender clear. He escaped on a plane but this plane most probably crashed. Due to this, Subhash Chandra Bose died on 18 August 1945.

Ideology of Subhash Chandra Bose

First of all, Subhash Chandra Bose strongly supported the complete independence of India. In contrast, the Congress Committee initially wanted independence in phases, through Dominion status. Furthermore, Bose was elected president of Congress for two consecutive terms. But due to his ideological conflicts with Gandhi and Congress, Bose took resignation. Bose was against

Mahatma Gandhi's approach of non-violence. Subhash Chandra Bose was a supporter of violent resistance.

Subhash Chandra Bose is an unforgettable national hero. He had tremendous love for his country. Furthermore, this great personality sacrificed his whole life for the country.

CHAPTER THIRTY-NINE

RANI LAXMI BAI

She was born to a Maharashtrian family at Kashi (now Varanasi) in the year 18 November 1835. During her childhood, she was called by the name Manikarnika. Affectionately, her family members called her Manu. At a tender age of four, she lost her mother. As a result, the responsibility of raising her fell upon her father. While pursuing studies, she also took formal training in martial arts, which included horse riding, shooting and fencing. To know the complete life history of Jhansi ki Rani – Rani Lakshmi Bai, read on.

In the year 1842, she got married to the Maharaja of Jhansi, Raja Gangadhar Rao Newalkar. On getting married, she was given the name Lakshmi Bai. Her wedding ceremony was held at the Ganesh temple, located in the old city of Jhansi. In the year 1851, she gave birth to a son. Unfortunately, the child did not survive more than four months.

In the year 1853, Gangadhar Rao fell sick and became very weak. So, the couple decided to adopt a child. To ensure that the British do not raise an issue over the adoption, Jhansi ki Rani – Rani Lakshmi Bai got this adoption witnessed by the local British representatives. On 21st November 1853, Maharaja Gangadhar Rao died.

She inspired many generations of Hindustani's, thus becoming immortal in the freedom fight. We bow before such a brave warrior, the Jhansi ki Rani – Rani Lakshmi Bai. The life history of the Jhansi ki Rani – Rani Lakshmi Bai, who preferred to sacrifice her life at the young age of 23 years in battle, is very inspiring. She surprised the British by showing extraordinary fighting spirit and valour in battles fought at Jhansi, then Kalpi and lastly at Gwalior. The British Major Sir Hugh Rose had to come down to treachery so as to be able to win over the fort of Jhansi. Such an extraordinary lady, who tied her son on her back while fighting the battle, will not be found in the history of the world. The valour and brave death she chose, which gave inspiration to the patriots belonging to the 'Gadar' party in the First World War, the organization of Shahid Bhagat Singh and to all revolutionaries from Swatatntryaveer Savarkar to Subhashchandra, is magnificent. Lot of literature has been written on the life history of Jhansi ki Rani – Rani Lakshmi Bai. Heroic poems have been composed in her honor.

CHAPTER FORTY

CHANAKYA

Chanakya is famous in the history of India as a sage-like person who by his political shrewdness and expediency helped in the establishment of the mighty Mauryan empire. Chanakya was wise, clever, foresighted, determined and deeply read in economics, diplomacy and politics. There is a legend that Chanakya was once invited to the court of the Nanda rulers of Magadha where he was insulted. Chanakya took a vow to cause the downfall of the Nanda dynasty. With the help of a brave and capable general, Chandragupta, he succeeded in fulfilling his vow and founded a new Mauryan dynasty in Magadha. He expelled the Greek invaders from India with his help again. Chanakya served as a friend, philosopher and guide to Chandragupta Maurya. Chanakya is also believed to be the author of Arthshastra, the classical Indian treatise on statecraft. It lays down rules of government and also gives a detailed account of the contemporary state administration.

Chanakya was born in a poor Brahmin family of Taxila. His real name was Vishnugupta. Chanakya is also known as `Kautilya' because of his `Kut-Niti' or diplomacy. He was educated at Taxila, a great educational centre in those times. In his personal life, Chanakya was like an ascetic and the legend goes that he lived in a mud-hut near the royal palace. A very famous Sanskrit play, Mudrarakshasa, has for its theme one of the diplomatic feats of Chanakya.

CHAPTER FORTY-ONE

NATURE

Nature has been in existence long before humans and ever since it has taken care of mankind and nourished it forever. In other words, it offers us a protective layer which guards us against all kinds of damages and harms. Survival of mankind without nature is impossible and humans need to understand that.

If nature has the ability to protect us, it is also powerful enough to destroy the entire mankind. Every form of nature, for instance, the plants, animals, rivers, mountains, moon, and more holds equal significance for us. Absence of one element is enough to cause a catastrophe in the functioning of human life.

We fulfill our healthy lifestyle by eating and drinking healthy, which nature gives us. Similarly, it provides us with water and food that enables us to do so. Rainfall and sunshine, the two most important elements to survive are derived from nature itself.

Further, the air we breathe and the wood we use for various purposes are a gift of nature only. But, with technological advancements, people are not paying attention to nature. The need to conserve and balance the natural assets is rising day by day which requires immediate attention.

In order to conserve nature, we must take drastic steps right away to prevent any further damage. The most important step is to prevent deforestation at all levels. Cutting down of trees has serious consequences in different spheres. It can cause soil erosion easily and also bring a decline in rainfall on a major level.

CHAPTER FORTY-TWO

GLOBAL WARNING

Global Warming is a term almost everyone is familiar with. But, its meaning is still not clear to most of us. So, Global warming refers to the gradual rise in the overall temperature of the atmosphere of the Earth. There are various activities taking place which have been increasing the temperature gradually. Global warming is melting our ice glaciers rapidly. This is extremely harmful to the earth as well as humans. It is quite challenging to control global warming; however, it is not unmanageable. The first step in solving any problem is identifying the cause of the problem. Therefore, we need to first understand the causes of global warming that will help us proceed further in solving it. In this essay on Global Warming, we will see the causes and solutions of Global Warming.

Global warming has become a grave problem which needs undivided attention. It is not happening because of a single cause but several causes. These causes are both natural as well as manmade. The natural causes include the release of greenhouses gases which are not able to escape from earth, causing the temperature to increase.

Further, volcanic eruptions are also responsible for global warming. That is to say, these eruptions release tons of carbon dioxide which contributes to global warming. Similarly, methane is also one big issue responsible for global warming.

it might be challenging but it is not entirely impossible. Global warming can be stopped when combined efforts are put in. For that, individuals and governments, both have to take steps towards achieving it. We must begin with the reduction of greenhouse gas.

Furthermore, they need to monitor the consumption of gasoline. Switch to a hybrid car and reduce the release of carbon dioxide. Moreover, citizens can choose public transport or carpool together. Subsequently, recycling must also be encouraged.

CHAPTER FORTY-THREE

PLANTS

Humans depend on plants in numerous ways. One reason we depend on plants is for consumption. Plants have the unique ability of producing their own food through a process called photosynthesis. In this process, plants are able to produce macromolecules such as carbohydrates that cannot be produced in animals or humans. In humans, the only to gain these macromolecules is to consume plant matter, or consume plant-eating animals (herbivores).

When humans consume plants, the carbohydrates, lipids, and proteins that are broken down through two forms of cellular respiration. The two processes of cellular respiration displayed in humans are anaerobic or aerobic. The deciding process used depends on the presence of oxygen.

This means that humans not only need plants for eating, but also need their created oxygen to break the food down efficiently.

In humans, cellular respiration also produces heat also needed in the body for thermoregulation, Thermoregulation that is an example of temperature

homeostasis in humans, requires heat energy to maintain a relatively constant internal temperature. All the heat energy that is needed for survival would not exist without plants.

Water is also a requirement in humans, and is needed for the body to balance fluid through osmoregulation. By consuming plants, the water that they contain will also be transferred to the consumer. An example of this could be in the consumption of coconuts. Coconuts usually contain a good supply of water. The water found in young coconuts contains electrolytes and a pH level similar to human blood. This could be beneficial by providing fast hydration and are normally found in warm tropical climates where hydration is a major concern.

Other then being used for consumption, plants also provide shelter from the environment. Trees provide shade, which creates a cooler temperature that helps prevent dehydration. They also provide fruit and shelter for animals for human consumption. Trees are also cut up into wood for building houses and making tools needed for hunting and protection from predators. Humans have an advantage over animals because of our greater intelligence that permitted the discovery of tools. Without

CHAPTER FORTY-FOUR

MONEY

Money is an essential need to survive in the world. In today's world, almost everything is possible with money. Moreover, you can fulfill any of your dreams by spending money. As a result, people work hard to earn it. Our parents work hard to fulfill our dreams.

Black money is the money that people earn with corruption. For your information corruption involves the misuse of the power of high posts. For instance, it involves taking bribes, extra money for free services, etc. Corruption is the main cause of the lack of proper growth of the country.

Moreover, money that people having authority earns misusing their powers is black money. Furthermore, these earnings do not have proper documentation. As a result, the people who earn this do not pay income tax. Which is a great offense and the person who does this can be behind bars.

Money Laundering

In simple terms, money laundering is converting black money into white money. Also, this is another illegal offense. Furthermore, money laundering also encourages various crimes. Because it is the only way criminal can use their money from illegal sources. Money laundering is a crime, and the people who practice it are liable to go to jail.

Therefore the Government is taking various preventive measures to abolish money laundering. The government is linking bank accounts to AADHAR Card. To get all the transaction detail of each bank account. As a result, the government comes to know if any transaction is from an illegal source.

Also, every bank account has its own KYC (Know your Customer) this separates different categories of income of people. Businessmen are in the high-risk category. Then comes the people who are on a high post they are in the medium-risk category. Further, the last category is of the Employee sector they are at the lowest risk.

White money is the money that people earn through legal sources. Moreover, it is the money on which the people have already paid the tax. The employee sector of any company always has white money income.

Because the tax is already levied on their income. Therefore the safest way to earn money is in the employment sector. But your income will be limited here. As a result, many people take a different path and choose entrepreneurship. This helps them in starting their own company and make profitable incomes.

Every person in this world works hard to earn money. People try different methods and set of skills to increase their incomes.

CHAPTER FORTY-FIVE

TIME

Time is very precious and we should not waste it in any way. Likewise, we can earn the money we spent but we cannot get back the time we have lost. So, this makes the time more valuable than money. Hence, we should utilize the time in the most possible way.

This the most valuable and precious thing in the world. Also, we should use it for our good as well as for the good of others around us. This will help us and the society to progress towards a better tomorrow. Moreover, we should teach our children the importance and value of time. Also, wasting time will only lead you to cause an issue to you and the people around you.

Although most people do not understand how valuable time is until they lost it. Besides, there are people in the world who prioritize money over time because according to them, time is nothing. But, they do not realize the fact that it is time that has given them the opportunity to earn money. Apart from this, the time has given us prosperity and happiness and on the contrary, it has also given us sorrow and grief.

Power of Time

In previous time many kings proclaim themselves as the ruler of their age and all. But, they forget that they have limited time. Time is the only thing in the world that is limitless. Time can make you a king or a beggar in a movement of seconds.

In conclusion, we can say that time is the greatest gift of God. Moreover, there is a saying that "if you waste time, time will waste you." Only this line is enough to justify how important and valuable time is.

CHAPTER FORTY-SIX

OXYZEN

Oxygen is basically a colourless and odourless gas which is a part of several compounds like water as well. Humans along with other mammals require oxygen necessarily. They need it to carry out their daily tasks and smooth functioning of the body.

Even the cells in our body need oxygen to function properly. All the living beings inhale oxygen in their lungs for proper respiration. After that, our cells absorb this gas to distribute it evenly to other cells of the body. Most importantly, oxygen is also stored in our body for emergency use so we can survive critical situations.

Furthermore, we also need oxygen to produce energy which helps in doing our tasks efficiently. For instance, through oxidation, our food and liquid get converted into energy. It is also beneficial in repairing our cells and maintaining our health.

Thus, we must ensure that we get an abundant supply of oxygen from nature. Do not cut down trees and clear out forests. On the contrary, we need to plant more trees. Similarly, do not pollute the air and hamper the oxygen quality. Avoid using personal conveyance and make sure to not leave a carbon footprint.

CHAPTER FORTY-SEVEN

WATER

Water is an essential source for the survival of living beings. It would be an understatement to say that we cannot survive without it. It is made after the amalgamation of oxygen and hydrogen. Just like oxygen, it is also colourless and odourless.

Water is found in abundance on the planet though not all of it is safe for human consumption. We have been using water for centuries now, however, it is limited. It does replenish but that process also takes time which we are not giving it.

Water is equally important as oxygen is for living beings. Each body part even the tissue and cell need water for proper functioning. It helps in regulating the temperature of our body. Moreover, it also enhances the circulation of blood and oxygen in our body.

Furthermore, water is very important for lubricating our joints. Our digestive system also needs water for proper functioning. Moreover, water helps in flushing

out the toxins from our body.

Similarly, our brain cells need water for proper functioning. We must drink sufficient amount of water for a healthy life. It will help in keeping you fit and fine for longer life. Thus, we must save water and use it wisely. Do not keep the tap running when not in use. Avoid dumping your waste into water and keep it as clean as possible.

CHAPTER FORTY-EIGHT

TECHNOLOGY

The word "technology" and its uses have immensely changed since the 20th century, and with time, it has continued to evolve ever since. We are living in a world driven by technology. The advancement of technology has played an important role in the development of human civilization, along with cultural changes. Technology provides innovative ways of doing work through various smart and innovative means.

Electronic appliances, gadgets, faster modes of communication, and transport have added to the comfort factor in our lives. It has helped in improving the productivity of individuals and different business enterprises. Technology has brought a revolution in many operational fields. It has undoubtedly made a very important contribution to the progress that mankind has made over the years.

The Advancement of Technology:

Technology has reduced the effort and time and increased the efficiency of the production requirements in every field. It has made our lives easy, comfortable, healthy, and enjoyable. It has brought a revolution in transport and communication. The advancement of technology, along with science, has helped us to become self-reliant in all spheres of life. With the innovation of a particular technology, it becomes part of society and integral to human lives after a point in time.

Technology is Our Part of Life:

Technology has changed our day-to-day lives. Technology has brought the world closer and better connected. Those days have passed when only the rich could afford such luxuries. Because of the rise of globalisation and liberalisation, all luxuries are now within the reach of the average person. Today, an average middle-class family can afford a mobile phone, a television, a washing machine, a refrigerator, a computer, the Internet, etc. At the touch of a switch, a man can witness any event that is happening in far-off places.

Benefits of Technology in All Fields:

We cannot escape technology; it has improved the quality of life and brought about revolutions in various fields of modern-day society, be it communication, transportation, education, healthcare, and many more.

With the advent of technology in communication, which includes telephones, fax machines, cellular phones, the Internet, multimedia, and email, communication has become much faster and easier. It has transformed and influenced relationships in many ways. We no longer need to rely on sending physical letters and waiting for several days for a response. Technology has made communication so simple that you can connect with anyone from anywhere by calling them via mobile phone or messaging them using different messaging apps that are easy to download.

Innovation in communication technology has had an immense influence on social life. Human socialising has become easier by using social networking sites, dating, and even matrimonial services available on mobile applications and websites.

Today, the Internet is used for shopping, paying utility bills, credit card bills, admission fees, e-commerce, and online banking. In the world of marketing, many companies are marketing and selling their products and creating brands over the internet.

In the field of travel, cities, towns, states, and countries are using the web to post detailed tourist and event information. Travellers across the globe can easily find information on tourism, sightseeing, places to stay, weather, maps, timings for events, transportation schedules, and buy tickets to various tourist spots and destinations.

CHAPTER FORTY-NINE

KNOWLEDGE

Knowledge is understanding and awareness of something. It refers to the information, facts, skills, and wisdom acquired through learning and experiences in life. Knowledge is a very wide concept and has no end. Acquiring knowledge involves cognitive processes, communication, perception, and logic. It is also the human capacity to recognize and accept the truth. Knowledge can be used for positive as well as negative purposes. Thus knowledge can create and destroy at the same time. One may use knowledge for personal progress as well as the progress of the community, city, state, and nation. Some may use it for negative purposes that may not only harm individuals but can also harm the community.

Knowledge is a success– In today's world without education and the power of knowledge, it is not possible to succeed in life or even keep up with the fast-paced life. It is not just enough to have knowledge on a particular subject to succeed but it is also important to have knowledge about how to use it effectively to succeed. One should have knowledge

about various aspects of a subject.

Knowledge can last for a lifetime and it impacts our growth which influences everything in our life from relationships to work. Knowledge is important for personal growth and development. We can gain knowledge on everything that we find interesting like any dance form, art, architecture, history or just about anything for our personal development. It makes us wise enough to independently make our decisions in life. But it is important to adopt a positive mindset to become a constant learner only then it helps us progress and achieve our goals.

CHAPTER FIFTY

HAPPINESS

Happiness is something which is difficult to describe in words. It can only be felt. Happiness is essential for leading a good life but unfortunately it is missing from the lives of most people these days. Different people have different ideas of happiness. Some believe that it can be found in money, others feel happy and content when they are in a good relationship yet others feel elated when they are doing well professionally. Here are essays on happiness of varying lengths to help you with the topic in your exam. You can select any happiness essay according to your need.

Happiness is a way of life and not something that can be achieved and kept. People spend their entire life running after happiness but end up dissatisfied. They are conditioned to believe that they will be happy if they get admission in a good college or if they secure a good job or if they get an understanding life partner. While all these help in building a good life which is essential to attain happiness however these alone cannot bring happiness. Happiness is something that comes from within and not from external things.

Happiness as per Buddhism

As per Buddhism, "Happiness does not depend on what you have or who you are. It solely relies on what you think."

Buddha believed that happiness begins from understanding the main causes of suffering. He has given an Eightfold path following which helps control the mind and ultimately leads to happiness. However, this is not a one-time task. This needs to be followed daily. The idea is to teach your mind not to dwell in the past or worry about future and to live in the present. The here and now is the only place where you can experience peace and happiness.

Buddha has been described as "ever-smiling". His portrayals mostly depict him with a smile. This smile comes from a profound composure from within. Buddhism states that true happiness can be attained by knowledge and practice to develop mental calmness and this can be achieved by detaching oneself from the needs, wants and passions.

Happiness as per Hinduism

As per Hinduism, happiness is attained by way of one's own actions, past deeds and the grace of God. Three types of happiness have been mentioned in the

Hindu scriptures. These are as follows:

Physical Happiness: Also known as Bhautik Sukham, this can be attained from a comfortable living, bodily pleasures and sensual enjoyment.

Mental Happiness: Also known as Manasik Anandam, this can be derived from a sense of fulfillment and satisfaction. It is a state in which as person is free from all sorts of worries and anxieties.

Spiritual Happiness: Also known as Adhyatmik Atmanandam, this can be attained when a person is able to come out of the cycle or births and deaths and make a union with self.

The ultimate aim of a living being as per Hinduism is to experience supreme blissfulness as a free soul in the heaven. The human beings can experience temporary happiness on earth by fulfilling their duties however permanent happiness according to Hinduism can only be achieved in the heaven by attaining liberation.

Printed by Libri Plureos GmbH in Hamburg, Germany

9 798887 042732